sundance
LITTLE BLUE
READERS

Flying Machines

Focus: Materials

PETER SLOAN &
SHERYL SLOAN

This is a glider.
A glider has no engine.
It glides in the air.

This is a seaplane.
A seaplane has floats.
It can land on water.

This is a passenger plane.
A passenger plane has
lots of seats for people.
It can take people
a long way, fast.

This is a transport plane.
It has large jet engines.
A transport plane can
carry a lot of cargo.

This is a helicopter.
It has a rotor.
A helicopter can go
straight up and down.

This is an ultralight plane.
An ultralight plane has a
small engine. It can
land on a short runway.

This is a fighter plane.
It has powerful jet engines.
A fighter plane can fly
very high and fast.